A collection of 50 beautiful mandalas by various talented mandala artists to suit a range of skill levels.

"Be yourself; everyone else is already taken."
— Oscar Wilde

"Be the change that you wish to see in the world."
— Mahatma Gandhi

"Darkness cannot drive out darkness: only light can do that. Hate cannot drive out hate: only love can do that."
— Martin Luther King Jr.,
A Testament of Hope: The Essential Writings and Speeches

"Imperfection is beauty, madness is genius and it's better to be
absolutely ridiculous than absolutely boring."
— Marilyn Monroe

"There are only two ways to live your life. One is as though nothing is a miracle. The other is as though everything is a miracle.
-Albert Einstein

"Fairy tales are more than true: not because they tell us that dragons exist, but because they tell us that dragons can be beaten."
— Neil Gaiman, Coraline

"I have not failed. I've just found 10,000 ways that won't work."
— Thomas A. Edison

"The opposite of love is not hate, it's indifference. The opposite of art is not ugliness, it's indifference. The opposite of faith is not heresy, it's indifference. And the opposite of life is not death, it's indifference."
— Elie Wiesel

"I am enough of an artist to draw freely upon my imagination.
Imagination is more important than knowledge. Knowledge is limited.
Imagination encircles the world."
— Albert Einstein

"You have brains in your head. You have feet in your shoes. You can steer yourself any direction you choose. You're on your own. And you know what you know. And YOU are the one who'll decide where to go..."
— Dr. Seuss, Oh, the Places You'll Go!

"It is never too late to be what you might have been."
— George Eliot

"There is no greater agony than bearing an untold story inside you."

— Maya Angelou, I Know Why the Caged Bird Sings

"Everything you can imagine is real."
— Pablo Picasso

"You can never get a cup of tea large enough or a book long enough to suit me."
— C.S. Lewis

"Life becomes easier and more beautiful when we can see the good in other people."
— Roy T. Bennett

"Life isn't about finding yourself. Life is about creating yourself."
— George Bernard Shaw

"Do what you can, with what you have, where you are."
— Theodore Roosevelt

"Success is not final, failure is not fatal: it is the courage to continue that counts."
— Winston S. Churchill

"When one door of happiness closes, another opens; but often we look so long at the closed door that we do not see the one which has been opened for us."
— Helen Keller

"Listen to the mustn'ts, child. Listen to the don'ts. Listen to the shouldn'ts, the impossibles, the won'ts. Listen to the never haves, then listen close to me... Anything can happen, child. Anything can be."
— Shel Silverstein

"And, when you want something, all the universe conspires in helping you to achieve it."
— Paulo Coelho, The Alchemist

"You may say I'm a dreamer, but I'm not the only one. I hope someday you'll join us. And the world will live as one."
— John Lennon

"It's no use going back to yesterday, because I was a different person then."
— Lewis Carroll

"It's the possibility of having a dream come true that makes life interesting."
— Paulo Coelho, The Alchemist

"What you're supposed to do when you don't like a thing is change it. If you can't change it, change the way you think about it. Don't complain."
— Maya Angelou, Wouldn't Take Nothing for My Journey Now

"A person's a person, no matter how small."
— Dr. Seuss, Horton Hears a Who!

"Well-behaved women seldom make history."
— Laurel Thatcher Ulrich, Well-Behaved Women Seldom Make History

"When I despair, I remember that all through history the way of truth and love have always won. There have been tyrants and murderers, and for a time, they can seem invincible, but in the end, they always fall. Think of it--always."
— Mahatma Gandhi

"Nothing is impossible, the word itself says 'I'm possible'!"
— Audrey Hepburn

"Do what you feel in your heart to be right – for you'll be criticized anyway."
— Eleanor Roosevelt

"I can't give you a sure-fire formula for success, but I can give you a formula for failure: try to please everybody all the time."
— Herbert Bayard Swope

"Never doubt that a small group of thoughtful, committed, citizens can change the world. Indeed, it is the only thing that ever has."
— Margaret Mead

"Peace begins with a smile.."
— Mother Teresa

"Happiness is not something ready made. It comes from your own actions."
— Dalai Lama XIV

"Whatever you are, be a good one."
— Abraham Lincoln

"May you live every day of your life."
— Jonathan Swift

"And once the storm is over, you won't remember how you made it through, how you managed to survive. You won't even be sure, whether the storm is really over. But one thing is certain. When you come out of the storm, you won't be the same person who walked in. That's what this storm's all about."
— Haruki Murakami, Kafka on the Shore

"First they ignore you. Then they ridicule you. And then they attack you and want to burn you. And then they build monuments to you."
— Nicholas Klein

"Attitude is a choice. Happiness is a choice. Optimism is a choice. Kindness is a choice. Giving is a choice. Respect is a choice. Whatever choice you make makes you. Choose wisely."
— Roy T. Bennett, The Light in the Heart

"Isn't it nice to think that tomorrow is a new day with no mistakes in it yet?"
— L.M. Montgomery

"You can't stay in your corner of the Forest waiting for others to come to you. You have to go to them sometimes."
— A.A. Milne, Winnie-the-Pooh

"Don't be pushed around by the fears in your mind. Be led by the dreams in your heart."
— Roy T. Bennett, The Light in the Heart

"Pain is inevitable. Suffering is optional."
— haruki murakami, What I Talk About When I Talk About Running

"Instead of worrying about what you cannot control, shift your energy to what you can create."
— Roy T. Bennett, The Light in the Heart

"When I was 5 years old, my mother always told me that happiness was the key to life. When I went to school, they asked me what I wanted to be when I grew up. I wrote down 'happy'. They told me I didn't understand the assignment, and I told them they didn't understand life."
— John Lennon

"Always do what you are afraid to do."
— Ralph Waldo Emerson

"In the end, we will remember not the words of our enemies, but the silence of our friends."
— Martin Luther King Jr.

"Fantasy is hardly an escape from reality. It's a way of understanding it."
— Lloyd Alexander

"If you can't fly then run, if you can't run then walk, if you can't walk then crawl, but whatever you do you have to keep moving forward."
— Martin Luther King Jr.

"Accept yourself, love yourself, and keep moving forward. If you
want to fly, you have to give up what weighs you down."
— Roy T. Bennett, The Light in the Heart

Made in the USA
Monee, IL
13 December 2022

21550212R00057